Dutch Proverbs

For the Concert of life,

No one

receives a Program.

Collected by Holly Flame Heusinkveld and Jean Caris-Osland
Hindeloopen Folk Art by Sallie Haugen DeReus
Graphic Design by Dana Lumby

Penfield
Press

Compiled by:
Holly Flame Heusinkveld traces her ancestry to Dutch immigrants who set-
tled first in Minnesota in the 1870s. She is a student interested in history
and literature.

Jean Caris-Osland graduated with a degree in Education from Iowa
Wesleyan College in Mount Pleasant, Iowa, her hometown. She is an asso-
ciate editor at Penfield Press in Iowa City and has contributed to several
Penfield Press books including *Dutch Touches: Recipes and Traditions*.

About the Artists:
Sallie Haugen DeReus is a folk artist whose beautiful Hindeloopen paintings grace the front and back covers of *Dutch Proverbs*. Throughout the
book are her sketches and designs in traditional Hindeloopen style. Sallie
lives on a farm in Mahaska County, Iowa, not far from the Dutch settle-
ment of Pella. Working from her summer kitchen turned studio, she has
been painting and researching Dutch folk art. In the early 1960s, Ms.
DeReus graduated from Iowa State University with a degree in Applied
Art and eventually traveled twice to the Netherlands to independently
study Dutch folk art in the museums of Friesland. Examples of Ms.
DeReus's Hindeloopen paintings can be seen in Pella, Iowa, in the
Historical Museum, Strawtown Inn and Restaurant, McDonalds
Restaurant, DePelikaan Imports and Pella Window Corporation. In the
Dutch community of Fulton, Illinois, they can be seen in the public library.

Dana Lumby, artist, with a degree in drawing and painting from Iowa State
University, created the page layout and artistic design of the proverbs.

Acknowledgements:
Professor Phil Webber, Central College, Pella, Iowa
Olga Burgerhout Tipton, Press and Cultural Affairs,
    Consulate General of the Netherlands in Chicago
Carol Van Klompenburg, author, Pella, Iowa
Esther Feske, graphic artist, Albuquerque, New Mexico
Robyn Loughran, graphic artist, Iowa City, Iowa

Edited by:
Dorothy Crum, Esther Feske, Diane Heusinkveld and Joan Liffring-Zug.

Origin of the Proverbs:
The proverbs in this book are principally from a *Polyglot of Foreign Proverbs*
by Henry G. Bohn, Bell & Daldy, 6 York Street, Covent Garden, and 186
Fleet Street, London, 1867.

Table of Contents

History of Hindeloopen

On what used to be the Zuider Sea in northwest Netherlands is the small fishing village of Hindeloopen. Glory days were in the seventeenth century when it belonged to the Hanseatic League. Hindeloopen was a thriving seaport, and traded as far east as China and as far north as Scandinavia and Russia. During this time, the ornate decoration of the Baroque and Rococco periods invaded the homes of the wealthy and middle class across Europe and Scandinavia. Guild and self-taught painters in every country lavished their decoration skills on painted wood surfaces such as furniture and walls in an attempt to brighten home interiors and add inspiration to their surroundings.

Hindeloopen villagers developed a distinct style of painting. Drawing from the scrolls of the Baroque period, the exotic birds of East Indian art, and the stylization of flower forms, the Hindeloopen painters came up with unique folk art forms. One form is the shadow painting that is characterized by light and dark strokes on a middle value, such as light and dark blue on a middle value blue background. Another form is the more transparent "porcelain" painting of light and middle-value blue on an off-white background. These two painting forms may have been the forerunner of the more colorful painting that followed. This later form is recognized by its red or green background, red being the most popular choice, varying from brownish-red to bright red.

The objective of the artist was to fill a space with decoration, be it a table leg, door panel or storage chest. Flowers and berries of varying kinds were painted in a stylized fashion. Motifs varied with the skill of the painter, but in general, stayed within a tradition that became recognized as Hindeloopen folk art.

The traveler who visits Hindeloopen today will find a thriving community of artisans who continue to make a livelihood by decorating furniture and other pieces in the traditional Hindeloopen folk art. Hindeloopen, Leewarden and Groeningen communities have fine museums with exceptional collections of Hindeloopen painted artifacts from the eighteenth and nineteenth centuries.

— *Sallie Haugen DeReus*

Experience

He that is
Embarked
with the

Devil

must Sail
With
Him.

Die met den duivel ingescheept is,
moet met hem overvaren.

He that
Despises
the little

is not

Worthy

of the

Great.

A roadside **Carpenter**
has many *Advisers.*

Thistles  and **Thorns** prick sore

but **Evil Tongues** prick more.

We hang Little Thieves, and let great ones Escape. ◆

No better Masters than Poverty and Want.

Whoever steals **Once** is a thief forever.

Whoever makes **NOmistakes** is doing **Nothing.**

Whoever has the Choice has the **Agony.**

Don't
Throw
Away

your old
shoes until
you have got
new ones.

Geen oude schoenen verwerpen
eer men nieuwen heeft.

An *idle* man
is the devil's pillow.

Better
half an egg
than an empty shell.

Rest,
Rust.

Crumbs,
too, are
Bread.

Seven
hours' **Sleep** are
Good
for One;

More than that is
Overdone.

If you sow no Grain, you harvest
Thistles.

A thread a Day
makes a shirt sleeve in a year.

Perseverance
brings
Success.

Even the best knitter

Sometimes

drops a stitch.

With the *Wind* behind, every sailboat can *Race.*

"Can't"
lies in the cemetery;

"Won't"
lies beside it.

Who undertakes many things
at once
seldom does anything well.

One is
Foolish
to live
Poor
and die
Rich.

Work
ennobles,
but Nobles
don't work.

Thrift with eager work builds houses like CASTLES.

Little is
done
where
many
command.

He who is not careful with little is not worthy of lots.

Wisdom

A *soft* answer turneth away Wrath.

Een zacht antwoord stilt den toorn.

The master wisely says,
"perhaps".

The student says,
"for sure".

It is
safest
sailing
within
reach of
the shore.

SHAME

lasts longer than poverty.

 *Everyone must row with the oars he has.*

An ounce of
Patience

is worth
a pound
of brains.

Een ons geduld is meer dan
een pond verstand.

Hunger
is the best Sauce.

The
Richest
Man, whatever the lot,
is he who is content
with what he has got.

Truth is Lost with too much
Debating.

In the land of

promise

a man may die of

 hunger.

*Hasty questions
require slow answers.*

Virtue

is its own reward.

De deugd beloont zich zelve.

❧ Honor ❧

Honor
Once*Lost*

Never
Returns.

Na eer en staat volgt nijd en haat.

No matter
how fast the **Lie,**
in the end
the truth will pass it.

After Honor
& State

follow envy & hate.

A man is not known
till he cometh to
Honor.

Men kent een man niet eer
voor dat hij komt tot eer.

In the
courtroom
of the
conscience,
a case is
always in
progress.

Nobility
of
Soul
is more
honorable
than
Nobility
of birth.

Silence

Silence answers much.

Zwijgen antwoordt veel.

Better to Speak **Sense** occasionally than Nonsense continually.

Silence and Thinking

never hurt anyone.

Much Talk
Little Action

Out of the
Abundance
of the
heart the
mouth
Speaks.

Silence
gives consent.

It is not
the hen that

cackles

most
that lays
most eggs.

It is good
speaking that
Improves
good **silence.**

Were fools
Silent
they would pass for
Wise.

Speaking is silver,

Silence is gold.

Spreken is zilver, zwijgen is goud.

Home

Your
own
Hearth
is
gold.

Eigen haard is goud waard.

To *marry* once is a duty;
twice a folly;
thrice is madness.

The bestTreasure
in a man's home
is a good wife.

He who takes his
Wife
along
never comes home too late.

Without
"Yours" and "Mine,"
life would be divine.

"Every bit helps to
lighten the freight,"
said the captain,
as he threw
his wife

overboard.

With family, **Walk.**

With strangers, **Talk.**

The **Apple** Does not land far from the Tree.

What parents *whisper*, their children **Shout!**

Where poverty
comes in the

Door

Love

flies out the window.

East, West.

Home

Is Best.

~ Relations ~

Better **Keep** peace than make peace.

Beter vrede houden dan vrede maken.

A guest always brings JOY,

either by his coming
or by his leaving.

A merry host makes merry guests.

The world's a
Stage;
each plays his part,
and takes his share.

Fools
are
free
all the
world
over.

Dwazen zijn vrij in alle landen.

Go Softly
and look afar.

He who digs a pit for another may himself fall into it.

When two quarrel,

Both
are in the
Wrong.

While
two
dogs
fight
over a bone,
a third
sneaks it
quickly home.

Better Twice Remembered
than once *Forgotten.*

No one can have

peace

longer than his neighbor

pleases.

Better Alone

than in Bad Company.

Forced love
does not *Last.*

Love
makes a
small bed
Wide.

Love
makes labor light.

Friends

A Good **Friend** *is better than* **Silver** *and* **Gold**.

Een goed vriend is beter dan zilver en goud.

A *good*
Neighbor
is better than a

distant
Friend.

A *Friend*
at one's
back
is a safe bridge.

Before you
make a Friend,
eat a peck of salt with him.

Every man's
friend
is every man's
fool.

Allemans vriend is allemans gek.

Nature

Blossoms

are not

fruits.

Bloemen zijn geen vruchten.

 **Painted** Flowers have no **Odor.**

Young twigs may be *bent,* but not old trees.

All **Clouds** do not **Rain**

Alle wolken regenen niet.

It's pleasant to look on the rain,
when one stands dry. ◆

He who would
gather honey
must Brave
the Sting
of bees.

There is a
REMEDY
for all things save Death. ◆

Faith

They who
don't keep faith with
God
won't keep it with
man.

Die aan God geen woord houd,
houd geen woord aan menschen.

One **God** *one wife,*

but many friends.

Time
is God's
and
Ours.

When God will not,
the Saint cannot.

When God means
to punish a nation,
He deprives its rulers of
Wisdom.

When **God**  *pleases,*
it rains with every wind.

The wicked shun the light
as the devil does the cross.

Help *yourself*
and God will help you.

Everyone for Himself,
God for us All.

Better once
in heaven
than ten times at the
gate.

Everything
has an end
Excepting
God.